SuR ENTERTAINMENT GbR

AF169023

# Encyclopædia Comédica

*A serious journey to funny realms*

non-fiction book in popular scientific terms

by

Benjamin Leuteritz

First English Edition

Impressum

© 2020 Benjamin Leuteritz

Cover and design: SuR ENTERTAINMENT GbR

Editing and typesetting: SuR ENTERTAINMENT GbR

Contact: noonelivesinheaven@gmail.com

Production and publishing: BoD – Books on Demand, Norderstedt

ISBN: 978-3-734-750373

*„Reality is already so comical that a person could not have thought it up any better."*

**Dr. Uwe Boll**

*„I used to think my life was a tragedy. But now I realize, it's a comedy."*

***Arthur Fleck alias Joker***

# Chapter overview I

About the lack of humour in forewords
*(page 10 to page 14)*
The playing with words and the acrobatics of letters
*(page 15 to page 17)*
The classic joke
*(page 18 to page 122)*
The remembering joke
*(page 23 to page 25)*
Slapstick
*(page 26 to page 30)*
Animalisticly good humour
*(page 31 to page 35)*
Irony and cynicism, the pillars of satire
*(page 36 to page 37)*
Observations, nothing is more funny than reality
*(page 38 to page 42)*
Black humor
*(page 43 to page 44)*
Situation comedy, humour for the sake of circumstances
*(page 45 to page 48)*
Frivolous humour, welcome below the groin
*(page 49 to page 51)*
The fourth wall, or why I'm talking to you
*(page 52 to page 54)*
Infantile humour and how to learn to laugh around the corner
*(page 55 to page 57)*
Redundancy, the end of humor
*(page 58 to page 60)*

# Chapter overview II

New combination of humour elements
*(page 62 to page 64)*
Humour in music
*(page 65 to page 67)*
Humour in movies
*(page 68 to page 69)*
Humour in literature
*(page 70 to page 73)*
Humour in computer and video games
*(page 74 to page 76)*
Humour in other cultures, that' s what the world laughs about
*(page 77 to page 79 )*
Humour of the future, we will laugh about it the day after tomorrow
*(page 80 to page 82)*
Memes, the humour of the Internet, or the new form of allusion
*(page 83 to page 84)*
The humour of humourlessness
*(page 85 to page 87)*
Humor from the other star, aliens laugh about it
(page 88 to page 90)
A few words about the English edition
*(page 91 to page 92)*
Afterword humour / Epilogue comedy / Closing gag
*(page 93 to page 94)*
After the afterword
*(pagee95 to page 97)*
This is (not) an acknowledgment /This is (not) an advertisement
*(page 98 to page 102)*

# Part 1

# The humour elements

# About the lack of humour in forewords

They say if you explain a joke, it stops being funny. If that's true, this will probably be the least funny book ever. Because it wants nothing less than to explain: What is humor and how does it work? Even more difficult than writing such a book is the question: How should you start a book about humor? With a joke? With a humorous preface? Does *that* do justice to such a serious concern as finding out what makes us laugh? I think it was my father who once told me in confidence that he had never experienced anything sadder than my attempt to explain the gaming joke "Who laughs last has the highest ping" when he didn't understand it. Given the inevitable fact that this book has to start somehow, and given the fact that my explanations cause sadness when they want to be funny, I'll try a humorless explanation this time, why all the prefaces (except this one) prefer to be funny.

When I sit down on the couch with a newly bought or an old gifted book - I put the steaming cappuccino on the table *next to me* and I don't let any other person *around me* - then I am about to make a self-imposed commitment: I trade about ten hours of my life for words. This self-imposed obligation grows with every word I consume, and by the second chapter at the latest, it has become an unwritten contract that I will definitely finish reading the book.

So these are the first words during which I put my imaginary signature on this contract. As long as I am at the preface, I can withdraw at any time. Later on I have to resign painfully. So the foreword has to be really hot, I want to be wrested. Meanwhile, the book must feel like a heroin sample that makes the promise to release more of it chapter by chapter in the next few hours.

So any author who really wants to be *read* and not just sit around in the shop windows, puts all his linguistic talent, quality and charm into the prologue of his story. I can only recommend to everyone who is looking for linguistic means, callousness, eloquence and word acrobatics to read one prologue after the other. They are real treasure troves of verbal condensation. Because a lot has to be said in a short time with just a few words.

By the way, I have followed my own recommendation, just before you ask. I have read all the forewords I could get and I have rarely laughed so much. Not because they were bad (well, some were, but there are always shadows), but because they were funny. No matter how serious and distinguish, how sad, melodramatic or even disturbing the rest of the content was to become, in the beginning there was always a joke. Because nothing makes the reader more likely to pull out his imaginary pen and sign the contract than when he was made to laugh in the first minutes.

Now I also know how I actually want to start this book. Before I ask what humour is and how it works, I ask: What does it achieve?

The answer: simply everything.

It makes it possible for me to clarify how we both - you, the reader and I - address each other: We use the polite form of address. After all, we both want to take the title of this book seriously.

At this point there is a discussion in the German version of this book about whether to use the word "you" or the word "you" to adress someone. Excuse me. In your language there is no difference. You use the same personal pronoun for both the polite form and the personal address. In German we have two different words for this, with the result that nobody knows how to address someone. Believe me, I envy you Americans sometimes.

Many authors find it difficult to build up a bond with their readers and miss the opportunity to take them on their mental journey. When I read a book in the field of popular non-fiction and the author doesn't pick me up by not knowing how to address me, I wonder what the author thinks, what the reader thinks, who wrote the book: A machine? (Phew, the sentence was long, but it makes sense. Read it again and leave out what is written in brackets the second time).

Does he not trust me to acknowledge that I know that he is just a human being (just like me), who is struggling for words to convince me of his opinion / his book world / his whatever? Or does he want to show me that his words have general validity, that they are self-evident and that he has only written them down like a medium?

Either way, I want to be honest with you, dear reader. My words have no general validity. They are nothing more than my systematically worked up observations of humour, which I have put into words myself.

And I can tell you that these words do not write themselves. I have to fight for each of them. Sometimes I delete sentences or I don't dare to read them a second time because I think they are bad and then - I delete them too.

Writing is hard work and writing about the probably most funny topic in the world - HUMOUR - is anything but funny. Nevertheless, I start and if you are holding this book in one hand because you are pulling out your pen with the other to sign your 10-hour reading contract with me, then I guess I have finished it.

I wonder if congratulations are in order at this point. Too soon? Maybe. But it still motivates me.

The fact that you are reading these lines right now and that at least the hint of a smile is visible on your lips motivates me to continue writing. In comedy, this is called achronic narration. Or was it paradoxical narration?

You know what? We'll figure it out together. Come with me. Our journey into comedy begins.

# The playing with words and the acrobatics of letters

At this point of the book it is time for a confession. I am neither English, nor American, nor Australian, nor do I come from any other country where English is the national language. So I am not a native speaker. Perhaps you have already noticed the many strange phrases and incorrect grammar. In any case, we have now reached a chapter in which I can no longer hide my shortcomings and my origin. You are now reading a chapter about puns that the author does not even understand or grasp. You, the reader, must take over the understanding for me. Will you do that? Thank you. Then let's begin.

The wordplay is probably the simplest and most common form of humour, as it is easy to produce and does not require much previous knowledge. Often it is enough to exchange the syllables of a word to make it smile or - as in the opening sentence of this chapter - just change the spelling to create a new meaning with the same pronunciation. Oops, I had to leave out the initial sentence in the English version, because I couldn't translate it. Just imagine such a sentence in English, okay?

In German it has almost become a sport to misunderstand English song lyrics in such a way that you transfer similar sounding words into your own language. The English "I've got the power" thus becomes the proper name "Agathe Bauer". Don't you think it's funny? We Germans love such nonsense.

Surely you've played around with words, twisted them, exchanged them or changed them in some other way.

This method of word acrobatics is especially effective when languages are mixed. In German, the English phrase "nobody cares" sounds just like our "nobody cleans up". Or the actor Johnny Depp sounds like "Johnny jerk" in German. Surely there are also German words that have a different meaning in your language. To my shame I must confess that I don't know any. Maybe you?

But as easy as word plays can be generated, it is difficult to transfer them into other languages, because they are created by the exploitation of a language and are therefore inseparably interwoven with the target speech.

This also applies to the supreme discipline of word plays: absurd constructions. One of the best known examples of this is: "Why is peter pan always flying? Because he never lands." The combination of dialect and literal interpretation thus creates a bizarre paradox, which is the humorous element.

We can therefore divide puns into three categories according to their origin. Classified by their artistic quality (ascending), they look like this: Exchanged syllables or words > changed content through altered spelling > absurdity through bizarre combinations.

Most word games arise spontaneously, out of a situation. Therefore, many people have the impression that you must either have a gift or a talent for such word acrobatics, or that you are not able to do so. But this is not true. Anyone can make good word games or create funny absurdities. The only thing you need is practice.

If you want to become a master of puns, make it a habit of dissecting every sentence. For the sake of those around you, do this only in your head at first. Swap syllables, leave out words, add new ones, change spelling and include colloquial phrases. In the beginning, not much of it will be really funny and certainly not good enough to make friends or colleagues laugh. But the more word games you make, the more you will get a feel for the nuances of your language. You will unconsciously recognize regularities and patterns and become better and better.

The only problem is that once you have started and experienced success (for example, if you ask what type of bee can't make up its mind and answer: A maybe), then the game with words becomes an integral part of your everyday life.

To turn around the words, you then can't stop anymore. What? That wasn't funny? Well, I'm still practicing.

# The classic joke

I must have been about four or five years old when I gained an insight that I still think about today (a few dozen years later). This insight was so profound for me that from then on I oriented most of my life towards it and am writing this book today (or at least this chapter, I will write the others tomorrow, I promise).

This insight was even so important for me that I accept to lose your attention with this much too long preface. Even now, when you are rolling your eyes in annoyance and just skim the words in front of your nose to get to the essential sentence, I still can't articulate it. Therefore I write it (in German this is a big linguistic joke. However, I have the feeling that its humour is lost in English. Sorry for that):

**He who laughs, doesn't hate.**

When in a threatening situation people suddenly laugh, the feeling of threat also vanishes. A person who laughs at us is not something we are afraid of and a person who makes us laugh is something we like.

Humour is a true all-rounder. It can reduce antipathy and build up sympathy, it can make people fall in love or make a boring situation funny. Humour is the saviour in need. Unfortunately, we humans in emergency or stressful situations are usually not very good at being funny. And that is exactly what the classic joke is for.

The classic joke is usually an anecdote, a short story or a script dialogue. If we can't think of anything in a conversation, we simply ask our counterpart if he or she knows the joke about Little Johnny, Chuck Norris, the situation with the doctor or the blonde. Okay, before you contradict me, I personally don't find any of these jokes funny.

Neither the little Johnny who asks his father if he can write in the dark, to sign up his report card (*cough), nor the blonde who becomes a brunette thanks to artificial intelligence (*double-cough) and certainly not Chuck Norris who can play Tetris on a Rubix cube. (triple...well, it's a little funny, albeit stupid and cheap.) Let's take a better example of bad humor and go for the doctor who is asked by a fat man how to lose weight quickly and answers: By shaking your head left and right. To which the fat man replies: All the time? The doctor: No, only when you are asked if you want to eat something.

Anyway, jokes are the first kind of humour a childhood person tries his hand at. After all, a joke doesn't require any *real* personal effort except for the recitation. You simply have to remember a joke when it is told to you.

By the way, have you ever noticed that as soon as a person starts telling a joke, suddenly everyone in the conversation wants to tell a joke, too? And then another... and then another. Yeah, have you noticed that? Well, then I'm reassured that I'm not the only one who feels that way.

On the other hand, I have also noticed that in situations in which you would like to tell a joke (for example, because someone in the discussion group has just told one), I can't think of any in a hurry.

I've probably heard over a thousand jokes in my life (about 10% of them were even good), but if you put a pistol to my chest with the words "tell a joke", only the worst ones would come out.

Maybe that's why I don't like most classic jokes. And maybe that's also why I'm going to end this chapter prematurely. Trust me, the next one will be more interesting.

But if you disagree with me and find the next chapter terrible, please stay here and read one of my favourite classic jokes. Otherwise, leave the joke out.

What? You haven't read the next chapter? Then let's go. But if you have already read the chapter to hear the promised gag (then shame on you because you didn't like the "remembering joke") and:

Three friends are sitting in a bar, a good Djinn appears and says: "I grant each of you three wishes. Let's go through them one by one and then I will fulfil them for you. No strings attached."

Brief surprise, then shrug of the friends, coupled with the decision to accept the offer.

The first friend begins, "I want a dream house."

The second friend thinks, *That's not a bad idea*, and he wants the same thing.

The third friend thinks, and thinks, and finally wishes that his arms would wiggle around like crazy.

And so the second round begins. The first boyfriend says, "I want a top model for my wife."

Friend number two thinks again: *Not a bad idea,* and wishes for a top model too.

The third friend thinks, and thinks, and finally wishes that his legs would also wobble around like crazy.

Round three, friend one says, "I want to be super rich."

Friend 2 (you've probably guessed it already) thinks that this is not a bad idea (again), wishes the same as the first friend...

...and then finally it's the third buddy's turn with his last wish. He thinks, and thinks, and wishes that also his head would wobble around like crazy.

The good Djinn fulfills everyone's wishes and the three friends agree to meet again in exactly ten years in the same pub to talk about whether the fulfilled wishes brought them good or bad.

No sooner said than done. The three meet again ten years later and friend one says: "That was brilliant. I have a great house, a great wife and I am rich. I couldn't be better."

Friend two nods and agrees with the first one. Both look at the third friend, who sits at the table with wobbly limbs and has trouble formulating an answer by rotating his head.

He says, "Hey guys, I'm starting to think I wished for shit."

End of joke. We Germans find that sort of thing incredibly funny. Odd, isn't it? You may now return to the chapter on slapstick. Or perhaps you'd like to go back to the "remembering joke"? You got me all confused now. Let's not think about it and just turn the page, okay?

# The remembering joke

Welcome to my favorite chapter. Here we are dealing with a humorous element, which requires patience and overview, but rewards the user with an appreciative laugh. I call it the *remembering joke*.

You know the following situation: someone makes a statement in conversation (in connection with the remembering joke, let's call this statement "anchor") that is likely to be memorable. The conversation then continues and after some time the anchor is raised by saying: "So much for the subject (statement)". This is the simplest form of the remembering joke, which you have most likely used yourself - perhaps even unconsciously - before.

Recently I noticed the recalling joke in the program of another comedian. I hope he won't hold it against me that he has to serve for this chapter now. It's about Kaya Yanar, the German-Turkish-Swiss What-You-Watching?-Star (that was a lot of hyphens. Sorry, it won't happen again.) At this point I notice that you probably don't know this comedian at all. Because he is only known in German speaking countries. Maybe the following anecdote will amuse you anyway.

In his program " Charm of Switzerland" there is relatively at the beginning a part in which Kaya tells how he attends a yoga class together with his girlfriend and makes himself an "Indian" (if you know the program, you'll get the joke, if not, you'll probably just frown) that he gets thrown out.

The story is funny in itself, but at the same time it serves as an anchor that we have to remember. The program continues, Yanar points out bizarreities of the neighboring mountain people in the staccato and relatively at the end of his program he comes to the point that he wanted to become a member of a Swiss community.

The community invited Yanar to get to know him. They wanted to find out whether he would fit in with them. One of the community members said at the interview: "We won't take him. I know him from yoga." Boom, there it is: the remembering joke.

On its own, the remark "I know him from yoga" is not funny at all, elicits at most a tired smile. But because of the anchoring, in which our German-Turkish-Swiss What-Watching-You-star (sorry, I couldn't hold back the hyphens again) was kicked out of the yoga class because he made the teacher furious with his India parody, the whole audience started to laugh.

And this was not one of those emotional laughs that come up quickly and end just as quickly. It was one of those appreciative laughter mixed with strong applause and respect.

You can generate exactly the same thing by setting anchors as often as possible and catching up with them at the right time.

The good thing about it is that you don't even have to know how the joke is going to end when you set the anchor. In most cases it is sufficient to let time pass and wait for an association. If you then use the saying "So much for the subject...(remark)", you have understood the essence of the remembering joke.

Another example (though perhaps not as good as Yanar's) comes from a comedian I really appreciate. In fact, of all comedians, I appreciate him the most. Maybe you have heard of him. In any case, in his book "Encyclopædia Comédica", this comedian also dropped an anchor in the preface, which he caught up again at the end of the preface ( strange formulation, at least in German).

If you have read the book, you know what I mean: The imaginary signature. At the beginning, this Leuteritz described the same in general terms, saying that by starting a book, the reader commits himself to a 10-hour reading contract. At the end of the beginning (again this strange formulation) this weird writing Benjamin Leuteritz demanded the signature from you. Boom, a remembering joke. And if I "remember" correctly, you even laughed at this point. Admit it. Not? Well, at least you had a smile.

# Slapstick

My best friend (and I really don't mean just any friend, but my best one) once asked me for something with a serious expression and a sound in his voice that didn't tolerate any contradiction. Of this something I'm not sure if I will actually do it if it becomes necessary.

He said: "When the day comes when one of us farts and the other one doesn't laugh, then the farting one of us has to kill the other one. Because then everything we do here has no meaning anymore."

Yeah, farting is fun. In the same way, it is always (and I mean "always" in the literal sense) funny when a man gets an object thrown into his crown jewels (is that what the English call crown jewels when talking about primary sexual organs in men? You probably know this better than I do) and he then writhes in pain.

You know what? I take back the literal "always". If I were that man, of course, the humorous element would be lost. But you know what I mean: Non-lethal violence inflicted on others is something people (whether they admit it or not) almost always find funny.

Why else should fail compilations on youtube have so many clicks? Or why tries the desperate father to make his child laugh by hurting himself? Clearly because it works!

We can't defend ourselves against this kind of humor. It is archetypal and is deep inside us. Of course we can cognitively deny the comedy of the fart from before (it wasn't *that* funny either), but we laughed anyway. And when it happens again, we will laugh again.

I used to think slapstick was funny because we were given something unexpected and laugh because we didn't expect the fail / the accident / the violence / the whatever. But the much clicked Fail Compilations on Youtube - which were mentioned above - taught me better.

Concerning them, I often know pretty well what's going to happen. If the title says "Fail" and the thumbnail shows a house demolition, then I know that this will not happen as the busting champion originally intended. And if the house does indeed collapse to the detriment of him and possibly even buries the nearby car (of the scatterbrained blaster) underneath it, then I find it not only painfully fitting but also funny. Although I knew it would happen.

So if it's not the unforeseen that makes us laugh at slapstick, what is it? After all, in Bud Spencer and Terence Hill movies we know that Buddy will hit his opponent from above with a clenched fist and Hill will trick his opponent with skilful jumps. It's predictable slapstick and still funny. However, it occurs to me that you probably don't even know these two punch-up actors. In Europe, the two Italians who made a name for themselves in the 60s with spaghetti westerns are very famous. You can think of it as a more modern and above all more European version of Laurel and Hardy.

In order to explain why this humour still works, I must once again bring up the crying baby who is made to laugh by the pain of the father.

A child develops what we call an ego-consciousness only at the age of about three years. Scientists assume that this is related to the use of language. After all, much of an adult's thinking is based on language. We do not necessarily think in images and contexts, but in words.

But a baby does not know words at birth. So it would not understand jokes, funny anecdotes or puns. Slapstick, on the other hand, would understand. This is due to the fact that slapstick events are not rationalized afterwards in order to extract the funny element (like a joke whose punch line you have to understand).

Rather, slapstick directly affects the ventral striatum of our brain. If the term ventral striatum doesn't mean anything to you, it is colloquially called a reward center. Slapstick ensures that this striatum releases hormones and messenger substances that give us feelings of happiness. The result: we feel good and laugh.

A cook serves his food, which was laboriously prepared in two hours, stumbles on the way, drops the food - *bang* - the ventral striatum releases messenger substances and - *bang* - we have to refrain from laughing so that the cook does not become even more sour than he already is due to his misfortune. (Do you actually use the word sour when you speak of angry? In German we do so.)

(At this point I thought about whether I should go one step further and write that the cook would then approach the taste of the lemon in his dish. But that was no longer funny on the second reading, so it was gone. But since I am so bad at cutting out, the unfunny joke - quite tricky - somehow stayed in. Clever, isn't it?)

Have you ever actually seen a Disney movie? Or a Marvel film? Yes yes, I know, it's the same thing. But have you ever noticed that the humour in the films of this company relies almost exclusively on slapstick? Yes? Well, I'm glad I'm not the only one who notices that.

What? You want to know why? It's obvious: no matter how clever or how stupid, how old or how young, how German, American or foreign someone is, he will laugh at slapstick. There is no need to assume knowledge, no culture and no heuristics. With slapstick, the laugher can be picked up almost for free.

So, if on your next date you don't know how to make your potential partner laugh because you can't think of a classic joke at the moment (why do you always forget them in stressful situations?!!), then why don't you just hit yourself on the head? You will be amazed how your counterpart reacts.

PS: Do not do that. Slapstick is primitive humor. You better memorize one of the good jokes from this book and recite it. I beg your pardon? This book has no good ones? You haven't even finished reading it! Go on to the next chapter and reconsider your opinion. I'll wait for you here.

PPS: When the German version of this book was published, it turned out that readers did not stick to the postscriptum, but to the previous chapter content. I would therefore like to emphasize once again: Do not do that. I do not assume any liability if you do.

# Animalisticly good humour

What do animals laugh at? Do animals laugh at all? Is humour exclusively reserved for us humans or are there other species that are able to extract something funny from an entity.

In this chapter you will learn something about my language once again. In German, a male cat and an hangover are one and the same word. We call it "Kater". One "Kater" visits me mainly in the morning after drunken nights, the other one usually lives in my living room and likes to leave grey hair everywhere he has been for a few seconds.

In this chapter we want to deal with the latter and make the former forgotten with a tablet (I just took it... should work in half an hour).

My tomcat, let's call him Bruno (on the one hand because that's his real name and on the other hand because it's a great name for a grey British Shorthair), this Bruno became my first victim during the research of this book to find out if animals have humour.

When I think about it carefully, my Bruno seems to suffer from a kind of split personality or at least to exist in two contradictory forms: Don't touch me, or I'll hit you Bruno, and caress me, or I'll hit you Bruno. At first, the two are not immediately distinguishable from each other, but after physical contact my painful hand recognizes relatively quickly which Bruno it is. But let's leave the bloody, chafed part of the chapter and turn our attention to Bruno (in the context of our research) for the funny part.

Imagine the following situation: I'm standing in the kitchen, preparing my dinner. My faithful Bruno is sitting next to me and watching the hustle and bustle. When my plate is well filled and I am about to leave, I misjudge the inclination of the plate (you probably know this) and a good part of the sauce of my dish makes itself independent and lands on the kitchen floor. I look down, I look up, I notice that my food is now too dry for me and I put it away unnerved.

Then my eyes fall on Bruno. He watched everything, even went back a millimeter when the sauce touched the floor, but didn't make a face. I now look at him and he returns my gaze.

If he were human, he would have laughed already. But he is not. He is a tomcat, who is looking at me with big eyes and who is probably just realising that if I don't want to eat the dry slop on my plate, *he* will probably make his move.

But did he laugh? Did he laugh at my misfortune? How would I even notice? Maybe cats only laugh inside, and the only way to find out if Bruno is really laughing is to connect him to electrodes and analyse his brain activity when the sauce falls down.

But would I even draw the right conclusions from the data material? And how am I supposed to connect my touch-shy cat to electrodes if he won't even let me pet him until he has sniffed my hand first?

So the observation of my Bruno does not help me any further. We humans are quite egomaniacal in a certain aspect. Since we *laugh* when we find something funny, we assume that species that don't laugh can therefore have no sense of humour.

However, besides laughter, there is another indicator for the possession of comedy: implied action. If an animal carries out an activity that is obviously meaningless because it serves neither reproduction, nor food intake, nor protection, nor any other basic animal or human needs, we can assume that the animal does so for pleasure. In other words: simply because it has a desire for it and feels enjoyment.

Although such activities are extremely rare in the animal kingdom, they do occur and thus prove that animals can also be funny. Here is my favourite example:

Ornithologists have discovered that crows, for example, have a great sense of humor. This has been noticed because we humans like to depict the target of humorous attacks by crows. From Klagenfurt (a typical German sounding place), there are often reports of cyclists being harassed by crows. The crows fly close to the bikers, frighten them, poop on their heads or perform other mischief.

In my opinion, this behavior does not allow any other conclusion than: crows love to shit on people or make cyclists fall. The attacks do not serve to provide food, they do not increase the crows' protection. On the contrary: the crow has to take a risk to annoy a person. The fact that it does it anyway is proof that it obviously enjoys its interaction with people.

If you are still not convinced that there is such a thing as animalisticly good humour, I will give you another example, which we can argue about afterwards if you like. The topic is monkeys.

Both chimpanzees and orangutans have been found to emit human-like gestures of laughter when they encounter slapstick.

For example, chimpanzees tend to tickle their newborns or partner during the act of love. Both the tickled person and the tickler (stupid word, maybe I'll exchange it, in German it's the same as clitoris) then start to laugh. So with monkeys it is very clear and also human-like when they show strange behaviour. Pardon? Oh yes, right, we wanted to discuss.

So you're saying that monkeys are a bad example of animal humour, because after all they are related to us humans. You know what, you're right! So let's try a third example, shall we?

Okay, here it is: In the South American rainforest, there are repeated sightings of parrot families where one parrot pretends to have lost the ability to fly. It then tries to fall off the branch, but at the right moment it feathers its fall (I am particularly proud of this bad pun, by the way. Did you get it? It "feathers". Yes yes, all right, I know. That was bad. It won't happen again. Just keep reading, and let's pretend the joke's been removed by my editor) Then the rest of the swarm starts chattering furiously. The interpretation is clear: The falling bird is the slapstick comedian and his family is the laughing audience. Fascinating, isn't it?

You know what, I think we should end the chapter here. That's long enough. But something about the look on your face tells me that you're not quite convinced. So, just for you, here's sample number 4:

Dolphins, just like dogs, have an anatomy that makes us humans assume that they would at least smile, maybe even laugh all the time. That both animal species can actually feel joy becomes clear when humans and dolphins or humans and dogs play ball together and the animal - seemingly without meaning - always brings the object back after you throw it away. Here we can at least assume playful joy. It becomes interesting, however, when the dolphin bumps the ball out of the human's hand or lets it hit the water surface in such a way that the humanoid playmate gets excessively wet. When the dolphin starts to roar afterwards, one thing is absolutely clear: the fishy mammal has just made fun of us.

# Irony and cynicism, the pillars of satire

Some people would say this book is satire. But it's not! After all, I don't make fun of humour, I use it to describe it. I do use ironic and cynical elements, but that doesn't mean that...

You know what? You're right. My book is satirical. Or can something be ironic and cynical without taking the stamp of satire? That's a tough question, and I think I have an answer.

If you come across a sentence or a thought in my book that you fully agree with, then of course it was meant seriously. But if you find something ridiculous, then it was satire. Yes, let's do it that way.

Let's start with something serious: what is the difference between irony and cynicism? Don't worry, I'm not going to quote the dictionary or the Brockhaus here, but rather provide an explanation or differentiation with just one word: pain. (Short pause in which you let the explanation sink in) Okay, judging by your furrowed forehead, this one word was probably not enough after all. Let us formulate it (for your sake): cynicism = irony + pain. When I am ironic, I make an inconclusive assertion or thesis that runs counter to reality. If I make this statement cynically, it is not only funny, but also hurts. Shall we agree on this definition, dear reader? Rhetorical question. You have no choice. So, let's continue.

After separating irony and cynicism, let's look at how and why they both work and form the supreme discipline (I'm not sure if I'm not using this word a bit too often) satire.

Here it is similar to the word plays. Absurdities and incongruities seem to be something we humans generally find funny. When I ask somebody how old he is and he answers: My name is Henry. Then it is funny and can be clearly assigned to irony. When an oncologist dies of cancer, it is cynicism. We know that we must not laugh about it, because cancer per se is something very bad. And above all we don't want to laugh about it because we feel sorry for the oncologist and then feel bad. After all, laughing at a dead person is very irreverent. Nevertheless, in this situation we cannot deny the cynical and therefore (unfortunately) funny element.

Because in both cases (Henry's and the oncologist's) things collide with each other that we would not have expected in connection. And here it seems to me to be different from the slapstick that has already been described in another chapter. The moment of surprise with information that we would not have expected from its nature seems to be the foundation of the comedy of satire.

# Observations, nothing is more funny than reality

Actually, it doesn't take a comedian to make us humans laugh. The absurdity of reality is a cornucopia of creativity. Or as you might put it: God prefers to watch black comedies and we are the protagonists.

Whenever I accidentally bump my head, stumble or have some other mishap, I think to myself: Dear God, I can only hope that you have just had a good laugh, so that at least one of us has had some fun. And the longer I live (which makes the counter of head butts and stumbles get bigger and bigger), the more I believe that God will never let me die. Because then he missed out on slapstick at its finest. Or God plans a big, brilliant closing gag with me, the punch line of which only he will get to see. I don't know.

Anyway, the gift of observation makes even the most humorless person a top comedian. You surely know people who simply describe point by point what happened to them the day before and the audience is holding their stomachs in laughter. And if you bought this book to be funnier and more humorous, then you probably know the opposite case:

You describe supposedly funny events of your last days or things you have observed and then look expectantly at the person opposite you, hoping to see that person snorting away. But then: nothing. Or at most a tortured grin, which both the sender and the recipient know is meant to be pitiful. But what have you done wrong? Why are observations from one person funny and not from another (you)? What is the difference?

First of all, we must divide observations into two categories: comparative observation and inherent observation. In the comparative one, it is relatively easy to generate a laugh, since the funny element is not necessarily the comparison itself, but the content of the compared.

Example: You notice that a process is very slow. To make it concrete: you are waiting for someone who is not coming. Full of humour, you write to this person who arrives too late: "The BER will be ready long before you finally arrive." Boom - guaranteed laughter, and without any effort. The advantage of the observational comparison is that the work has already been done for us. The administration of BER has worked hard over the years to ensure that the simple mention of BER in connection with delays, inflation, mismanagement, etc. is already a funny element.

I guess you can't do much with the term BER unless you read German news. So here is a short explanation: In our capital city (Berlin) a new airport should be built, many years ago. And for many years it has still not been completed - thanks to considerable mismanagement, enrichment and pure incompetence of the involved parties. Believe me, in Germany the term BER has now become a dirty word.

But let's go on and talk about comparative observation. Here it becomes more difficult than with inherent ones.

Let's stay with BER for the sake of simplicity. If I were simply to read the bullet points of the development of this airport, it would probably only produce moderate humour. The absurdity of the miscalculations is also evident, but not enough to produce real laughs and not just smiles.

The observation must therefore be edited to make it funny. And now comes the part where you have to listen carefully if you want to make roaringly funny observations in the future. Remember two words: simplicity and placidity. Yeah, I know, that was three. Just leave out the "and," okay?

For an observation to be humorously tangible, it must be broken down to its core. Identify the essence of what you see and verbalize it. This is step one (simplicity). Then comes step 2 (placativity). Here you have to find out the meaning or interpretation of the observed and break it down to a cliché or stereotype. The result is a trenchant observation that will make you laugh with benevolence.

Too complicated? Right, I agree. So let us extract an example of the inherent observation: What follows is a true story. It must also be true, otherwise I would have to expect legal reprisals if I had made it up.

Surely you know the Deutsche Bahn? That's right, you're not German. In this case: Surely you know Amtrak? The following is the German equivalent of Amtrak. (in the best case I already got a laugh from you now, because your "comparative humour" spits out trigger words like delay, strike or similar things).

Here's what happened: I booked a trip to Switzerland, several months in advance. The railway company charges huge sums for trips that are booked at short notice. Early bookers, on the other hand, receive substantial discounts. A few days before departure I try to print out a travel plan. It doesn't work, the screen says something about "technical problems". Probably this is the most common word combination in Amtrak (Deutsche Bahn) texts.

So I write an email and ask for information when I should take which train. The days pass by, an email does not arrive, but the departure date does. Somehow I manage to catch the right trains and arrive (what a miracle) on time at the destination station in Switzerland. When I get WLAN in the hotel, I open my email program and - tada - (you probably guessed it already) the train sent me an answer in time for my arrival.

Summary: We have no idea which train you have to take. Please have a look for yourself.

Well, thanks for the conversation. Most useful mail ever. (By the way, I answered exactly that - without greeting and without saying goodbye - I thought it was fitting).

If I did everything right, you gave my words at least a smile, maybe even a broad grin in the last seconds, because I already did the transfer of simplification and placativity. In fact, my anecdote would have been somewhat less funny if I had reproduced it completely and without reflection.

Now follows the version without transfer service: The booking of the ride really existed, and it was done very early to get the super saver price. If I had been clever, I would have printed out the travel plan already on the day of booking and would have adjusted in the train app to inform myself in case of any changes of the schedule. I did neither of these things. It happened as it had to happen: the railway changed the timetable and my booked trip was consequently no longer findable in the system. When I wanted to see the detailed timetable shortly before departure, the rail service tried to access information that no longer existed. The consequence: "Fatal error. Please contact support." That's what I did. Result: Please inform yourself about track and train number on the spot.

As you can see, in the real story I am even partly responsible for the misunderstanding. The railroad company shows *concentrated competence* also in this version, but comes off a little better than in the previous one. And the most important thing: the second version does not really make you grin, and certainly not laugh.

To tell observations really funny, they have to be prepared as described above. To find out how you can best tell your own stories, simply invent several versions, present them to different people, and compare which stylistic devices were laughed at most and which ones made your counterpart look down in shame to avoid eye contact with you. Over time, you will develop a sense of how to stage stories to make them work. And when you have reached the pinnacle of observational comedy, even the most boring anecdotes are likely to be told by you.

# Black humour

Probably this whole chapter will be deleted by my editor. I don't know what color it will be, but it will be canceled. By the way, in German this is a big gag, because the word "delete" and the word "paint" are one and the same thing. Unfortunately, you miss this joke in your language. But it doesn't matter, because (of my editor) you will never read it anyway.

That's annoying, because you won't get to know this interesting fact about the German language. If you could see me now: I'm clenching my fist towards the editor. But I can't blame him, after all black humour lives from provoking, coming across as politically incorrect, insulting people, denigrating them or simply being mean.

When I went to black humorous sites like 9gag, 4chan or others for research purposes, one sentence especially stuck in my mind: "My humour is so black that it could pick cotton." I think that describes the dark side of comedy quite well and at the same time explains why this chapter will never see the light of the bookshop. Which is actually a pity, because I think the linguistic picture with the light of the bookshop is really felicitous, but what can you do? You will never get to see it.

Now that I'm all alone and I'm writing a chapter without you, my dearest reader, I might as well get the hell out of here and get a few things off my chest. I'm going to have a kind of soliloquy about black humor. That should be fun. I'll start:

First of all, I've noticed that black humor brings out a different kind of laughter in people than the other humor types. While "normal" laughter usually takes place in the high-frequency range and thus can be assigned to the head voice, black humour seems to cause a deeper, throatier laughter.

In the form of words this is quite difficult to convey, but for your sake I will try anyway. I beg your pardon? You're not there anymore? Oh, yes, right. I' m talking to myself. I'd forgotten again. Where were we? Oh yes, the explanation.

We can attribute the onomatopoeia "hihi" to normal laughter. But in black-humored laughter, it's a "hoo-hoo." Now do you know what I mean by frequency? No? Wait a minute. I thought you said you weren't here. Don't confuse me. I can't be distracted by you. You who are not here and will never read this chapter.

# Situation comedy, humour for the sake of circumstances

When I was a little boy, the greatest thing for me was to spend time with my grandparents. They had my favorite food, TV as much as I wanted, a big sandbox, lots of animals (guess right, my grandparents had a farm) and most important of all: no tasks and no rules.

The time at grandma and grandpa's place was just great. Sometimes I wish I could turn back the clock and experience everything again. Maybe that is also the reason why you have to torture yourself with this once again too long introduction: As I write about my grandparents, I feel like I'm with them. By the way, this is also the reason why I address you, dear reader, so often. I want to know if you're still here. I want to write the book together with you. I don't think I could do it alone.

But let's get back to the subject. My grandfather, unfortunately already deceased, but still deep in my heart, was probably the funniest and most humorous person I have ever met. In a way, he is my inspiration for humour. Not only did he always have a funny saying for every situation, he was also able to resolve conflicts through humour. Maybe it is unfair that my grandfather is only in this chapter. After all, I learned a lot about the structure of jokes from him. But in one point he unconsciously taught me much better than in the field of jokes, namely situation comedy.

I think I was eight or nine years old when this happened: My grandfather and I were watching television. If you (like me) are over 30, then you remember that. It's this thing with channels and schedules and above all: with advertising. Anyway, our program was just replaced by this so-called advertising and that was the sign for us to change the program.

Or did you (you, who are over 30) actually watch commercials or were you also one of the people who used the break to go to the fridge or to watch what the other channels have to offer? Well, I wouldn't have expected anything else from you.

Grandpa and I were one of those people who wanted to see what was going on on the other channels. Since I had read the TV guide (another thing from the distant past. In former times the programs of the channels were actually immortalized on uprooted trees), I knew what was going on on the other channels. I can't remember exactly which channel Grandpa (who was always the ruler of the remote control) should switch to. But I do remember that he had to enter a two-digit number for that.

Let's assume for the sake of simplicity, he had to switch from channel 6 to channel 12. How do you do that? Sure, you press 1 and then press 2 and you're on channel 12. It wasn't like that with us. My grandfather looked at the remote control, pressed 1, looked at the same control again and then pressed 2. When he noticed what he had just switched on, he asked incredulous: "THAT's what you want to see? This is bullshit." I said, "No, Grandpa, I don't want to see that. This isn't Channel 12, it's Channel 2."

You, as an observant reader, must know what happened. While Grandpa was looking for the Two, the One was already tuned in.

He, on the other hand, says, "Bullshit. I pressed one and two. This must be 12." So I thought I'd roll my eyes so Grandpa wouldn't see. Then, "You have to press faster," I say. "Much faster."

Grandpa looks at the remote again, finds one and presses it. Then another study of the keyboard, followed by another delayed pressing of key two. The channel changes, Grandpa looks at me and says: "Now it's right, isn't it?"

I feel like screaming and laughing at the same time. I say, "Let's see if the commercial's over by now."

Situation comedy works something like this. Meanwhile, the structure of this joke has been "stolen" from me by the American mockumentary series Modern Family (Yes yes, not stolen, it was only abstracted), in which a son gets upset about his father because the father does not double-click with the computer mouse, but (due to his slowness) two clicks. But I think my anecdote is better. What do you think? Do you agree with me? Great, then you have earned another example of situation comedy.

When I was in a former life (meaning a former job, but I'm sure you already knew that) at a seminar with overnight stays in a hotel, the following happened to me:

I visited one of my colleagues, with whom I got along best, late in the evening for a drink. As I staggered out of the fellow's room, I walked across a long corridor, looking for my place with the cuddly bed in which I would wake up the next morning hungover. (At this point the pun with the hangover and the tomcat would have come again. Be glad that you don't have to put up with it a second time, unlike the German readers). On the nightly way back to my room a door in the corridor suddenly opened and one of my colleagues - Hank - appeared. Confused, he asked: "Benny, what are you doing here so late?"

I looked at the number of the room he was coming out of and noticed that it was the room of our blonde, single parent fellow student, and looked at Hank again. "Nothing. And you?", I asked.

He looked at me and his relatively light skin turned red like a tomato. I didn't get an answer and we both stood there embarrassed for a few seconds. Then I said: "Good night Hank, see you tomorrow morning."

A smile spread across Hank's face and he shouted a relieved "Thank you, I wish you the same" as I left.

# Frivolous humour, welcome below the groin

And welcome to the chapter I like the least. I wouldn't actually blame you if you left it out here. So skip. ...

Stop! I'm just kidding. Stay here, please. That was irony. I know, it's a different chapter, actually. But you'll notice I try to avoid frivolity. That's why I beat around the bush.

But I'm running out of things to say. I seem to have no choice but to roll up my sleeves, pinch my ass cheeks together and give you a basic course in frivolous comedy. Let's go!

However, I must warn you. I'm not going to bother with this chapter. Faecal jokes and sexist gags just don't deserve to be elaborated on cleverly. In my opinion they are the bottom of the humor and that's exactly how I'm going to treat them.

Actually, we could almost end the chapter already. You already know the most important three points: Point 1 is faecal jokes (practically all jokes related to bodily fluids and excretions, *disgusting). Point 2 are sexist jokes (practically all jokes in connection with gender specification, *double disgusting). And point 3 is: Do not use this kind of humor. Just leave it out. Nobody will miss it. At least not me.

Remember that frivolous humor is the lowest form of comedy and will not make your counterpart laugh, but will show him whose mind you are. You won't cause laughter, but only give (negative) information about your intellect.

I once took the time to analyze comedies (in the field of film) in terms of the nature of their humour in relation to critical voices and found something amazing (or maybe not so amazing):

Comedies whose IMDB score was below 5 points, or in some cases well below 5, were usually shouted at: "If you like it frivolous, this is the right place, everyone else: Hands off!" Almost never were remembering jokes, humorous observations or pointed comparisons denounced. It was always the frivolities.

When I was five years old, I could still laugh about terms like vomiting, shitting, jerking off, fucking etc. (So, now I've worked through the most important words that must occur in a chapter on frivolities. Believe me, writing these words caused me physical and psychological pain). And even though I am now over 30, I would still describe myself as an infantile person.

For example, I can laugh about it when someone tells me I would be insane if I jumped from the bridge into the river in Paris. (Think about that for a moment.) French and Germans don't like this childish pun, they might not even understand it. I hope you find it amusing.

Nevertheless, I have lost the ability to laugh about the above mentioned terms (no, I will certainly not repeat them at this point). Some joke structures are just timeless, others are outdated. Frivolities definitely belong to the latter.

# The fourth wall, or why I'm talking to you

Do you know Deadpool? Okay, you've heard of him, but you haven't seen the movies. Doesn't matter. You haven't missed much.

Anyway, this Deadpool is one of those superheroes who jump across the screen in high-budget, mostly meaningless Hollywood movies, packed in tight tights and equipped with the cheapest jokes that were on offer.

Yes yes, you know these super, water, wonder and bat men and women. I'm afraid I know them too. Well, the last one is actually pretty cool. The others not so much. But, as is so often the case, I'm straying from the subject.

The difference between Deadpool and the other pantyhose men and women is the breaking through the so-called fourth wall. Instead of exclusively interacting with other protagonists, Deadpool violates the highest rule of filmmaking (never look into the camera!) and addresses the viewer directly. This is called the fourth wall, because in classic television, three-wall sets are usually built and the "fourth wall" is occupied by the audience. Very often this constellation is found in sitcoms or late night shows.

You've probably noticed it by now: I have a weakness for the fourth wall (as well as for the fourth estate, we scribes stick together) and I can't help but use this stylistic device far too often.

Believe me, I know that you have rolled your eyes at one time or another in this book and thought: "What does this guy actually want from me? Why is he always chattering at me. I thought reading was a one-way street." But I find it so much more personal and above all much funnier, because the fourth wall allows me to work through dry and very technical topics in a humorous way.

Let me tell you about my first encounter with the fourth wall. I guess I was about twelve years old when I read my very first Stephen King novel and swore to myself that one day I would read everything from this master of horror. The book itself read normally (if you can even use that word in connection with Stephen King). I think it was one of those short story volumes, "Nightmares and Dreamscapes" was the name of it, if I remember correctly.

Anyway, the short stories were followed by an epilogue written by the master. And this afterword became a revelation to me. I couldn't believe what I was reading: Stephen King, arguably the greatest and most important author of the present (opinion of the author of this book) spoke directly to me. He talked to me, so to speak.

It felt like I was having a private, almost intimate conversation with him, which he had written just for me. The art of course lay in the fact that SK knew exactly what I was thinking at each sentence and referred to this thought. It was almost as if King was sitting in my head and knew what was going on inside me. I was infinitely flashed. From then on, I wanted to harness the power of the fourth wall and I can only recommend that you do the same. (Unless you hate all the things I write in brackets. If so, leave out the fourth wall and avoid what I write in parentheses. Do you agree with that? Oh, right.)

# Infantile humour and how to learn to laugh around the corner

Children are easily made to laugh, is the prevailing opinion. If you want to irritate the diaphragm of an adult, you have to make an effort. But why is that supposed to be the case? Why is it enough for a child to use a strange-sounding word (like the city of Seattle, for example), while the same is something completely normal and unfunny for an adult?

The difference lies in the cognitive performance that has to be provided in each case and in the number of already connected and established neurons and nerve tracts in the brain. Let's start with the latter: The less input a brain has received in a lifetime, the more intensively it has to classify, process and categorize stimuli. As a result, the respective inputs feel new and fresh and are more likely to trigger emotions than when similar or the same information has already been received and routinely processed many times before.

You can explain it roughly in such a way that a joke becomes less and less funny the more often you hear it. The first time it is new and fresh, the tenth time it is corny and annoying. We humans must always get new information and stimuli so that we don't get bored. The problem: At some point we know most of the simple joke structures, even expect them, and therefore cannot laugh about them anymore. By the way, this is the same phenomenon that is responsible for our subjective perception of time becoming faster and faster the older we get. For a child, a year is almost a lifetime and holidays feel like months. For an adult (at least that's how I feel) the years just fly by and sometimes you don't know exactly how old you are.

Let's come to the cognitive performance quantum, which is necessary to process jokes. The absolute intelligence of a child (not to be confused with the relative, so-called intelligence quotient or IQ) is on average much lower than the absolute intelligence of an adult. As a result, an adult is more likely to be able to think through several abstraction steps, while a child usually has not yet mastered the art of "thinking around the corner". And this is exactly where the difference between infantile and adult humour lies: infantile humour touches directly and inherently from a situation. Adult humor requires at least one, if not several degrees of abstraction.

I would like to give you - as always - an example of this: A child can be made to laugh just by seeing a person stumble. Take, for example, the short film "Dinner for One", which is part of the good New Year's Eve tradition in many households. (At least that is the case here in Germany. Is it the same with you? Ah, interesting. I guess we have that in common). When Freddie Frinton stumbles over the tiger's head, a child is able to find this circumstance inherently funny. It doesn't need to know the plot of this slapstick interlude to laugh. For us adults (I guess you are one. At least you look quite grown-up, if I may take the liberty of saying so) the comic element, however, only arises through context sensitivity. We know that Frinton doesn't have to take just *one* alcoholic drink per course, *but many*. And we adults know that such amounts of alcohol lead to drunkenness and thus to a reduction of motor skills. So we do not laugh at Freddie's stumbling as such, but at the consequence of the constraints he is under. To this end, we have provided a cognitive abstraction in advance, which a child is usually not capable of performing. The more "adult" our humour becomes, the more diverse the degrees of abstraction and the number of corners we have to think around.

# Redundancy, the end of humor

Do you know these comedians who have been telling the same jokes for decades and maybe used to be funny in the past, but today they only seem embarrassing and shameful? Let us not mention any names for the sake of honour, but you surely know who I mean. Or rather, this definition applies to a whole range of people who were fresh and original at the beginning of their careers, but who today are stewing in their own - not at all funny - juice and simply tell old jokes in a not at all new way.

How would you rate *my* humour if in ten or twenty years' time you were to read the eleventh book I've written and you still found sentences like "this idea will certainly be deleted by my editor" or "let's argue about it together, dear reader"? You would probably think: "This Leuteritz is still pulling that thing with the fourth wall and thinks it's funny. It's kind of sad." Or you'd think, "He can't do it." And you'd follow up with, "Could he *ever*?" Was he funny *at all*, or a dilettante from the start?

The jokes of good comedians are like the David Bowie albums: Varied, sparkling, and always something different and surprising. The comedians described above, stewing in their own juice, can rather be compared to Motörhead albums: The first one was good and from the second one on there were only reruns.

And that is exactly the point. Please don't get me wrong, I like Motörhead and I also listened to the last CDs released before Lemmy's death. But if we are honest, their songs were not very different from their first songs. Nevertheless it is good music.

But if a comedian releases a only slightly different program every year and basically performs the same joke structures in a similar way (maybe with different names of the protagonists and a different setting), then the humorous effect unfortunately wears off.

Actually, we didn't want to mention any names in this chapter. For the sake of honor, I think you said, dear reader. But to be more specific, I have to give you an example. Since I don't want to get too close to any comedian who is still alive, I'll use an example that is already a bit older: Buster Keaton. If you spent more time in the last millennium than in this one, you may have heard of him. He was not only the first American to be given the first name "Buster", but also one of the silent movie stars of the early 20th century. His humor was largely a slapstick. With a stoic face he endured all kinds of physical reprisals and made the audience laugh (first as a wandering showman, later as a film actor). At some point this humour was no longer in demand. Affected comedians like Chaplin or Laurel and Hardy established a new kind of humor. Buster Keaton fell into a hole and the legitimate question arose: If his films are no longer funny now, were they funny at all? The answer: Yes, they were. But the merciless cogwheel of repetition ground them to dust.

Of course there are jokes that get funnier the more often you hear them. Much of this effect, however, is imaginary or has to do with one's own attitude towards the humorous entity. Much more often it is like the infantile humour described in the previous chapter: Jokes make connections between our synapses. If the same connections are used again and again without the need for new combinations, we feel bored and irritated. Therefore it is the first duty of every comedian to question his own concept again and again and to link the used humor elements again and again. So let's move on to the second part of this book at exactly this point; the practical application.

# Part II

# Humour elements in practice

# New combination of humour elements

Welcome to the second part of the book, where you will learn how humour elements are used in different media and forms of presentation. You will find that you already know all the basic principles. The only thing that matters is the abstraction to the relevant topic and the new combination of the underlying humour elements.

Imagine humour as a quantum-mechanical process in which each particle represents a basic structure. Depending on how these particles interact and combine, completely different constructs are created. If you only look at the individual constructs, you see such a variety that it is difficult to find common ground. But if you look into the smallest particles of the construction again, you will rediscover the modular elements.

Theoretically, it would be possible to develop an algorithm that is filled with all content-free humor elements and which - once you have fed it with topics and relations - creates random new combinations and thus writes jokes automatically. If you then also evaluate each joke afterwards so that the optimization algorithm can decide which combinations worked well and which less well with the given content, the whole thing would even be a self-learning system that gets better and better with each joke written.

If you, my faithful reader, belong to those computer scientists who like to code in their spare time, you now receive from me the solemn order to try out such an algorithm. You can send it to me via the email address in the imprint.

Pardon? This book is too thin and the humor elements are too few and not elaborated enough? You need more data material to create such an algorithm?

Then it is time to make a confession to you. The title "Encyclopædia" is a "joke" in two ways. You won't find *all* the humorous elements here and you won't have a comprehensive, complete reference book in your hands. Rather, what I have written is intended to spur you on to discover new elements yourself.

Cheap trick, you say now? You want your money back? Wait a minute, please. Let me explain. When you think back to your school days, what do you remember most? The factual knowledge that the teacher smeared on the blackboard in the smallest font and that you dutifully transferred into your notebook, or the one idea that made you think? Maybe it was sometimes just a word, a push, a thought to get the merry-go-round in your head going.

It may not be the best example, but I just remember a biology lesson in the 6th or 7th grade. If I think back correctly, the subject was metabolism. One of my classmates raised his hand during the lesson and asked our teacher if it would not mean immortality if you always supplied your body with exactly the substances it needs for a perfect metabolism. After all, the system could never fail and the cycle would continue. Our teacher dismissed the idea and told us about vegetative atrophy, only to return to the various metabolic processes afterwards.

If you would ask me today (or even just a few days after the lesson) about terms like biotransformation, assimilation or catalyzing enzymes, my answer would consist of a tortured grin and the hope for a change of topic soon. But the thought about the eternal circulatory system has remained. I can always check the facts on Wikipedia or even "enjoy" them in a prepared YouTube video. But my chain of thoughts about immortality would not have existed without this one idea of my classmate.

So in the following chapters I will not give you fact for fact and information for information. You won't be presented with anything to learn by heart, but you will get a cornucopia of ideas, which hopefully will give you as intense a train of thoughts as I had after my biology lesson.

# Humour in Music

I practically grew up with classic songwriters like Joint Venture, Gunther Gabriel or Helge Schneider. The humour in their songs is so funny and accurate in places that it almost makes me forget that classic songwriter music is not really my thing. I like it more rocky, with electric guitars, a drum set and all that. But again I digress from the topic. Besides, you probably don't even know the artists mentioned. You can compare them to your Steve Martins, Rodney Carrington's, Jimmy Fellon's or the legend Tom Lehrer.

Humour in music, of course, lives from the same humour elements that appear in classic jokes, sketches or puns. The difference, however, is that musicality adds two further dimensions: timing and broken or serviced expectations.

Let's start with timing, not only because I mentioned it first, but also because it almost explains itself. A song usually consists of two or three verses, a chorus and so-called bridges between them. It is ruled by principles like rhythm, beat, melody and tempo, which can change within the song.

The humour (if it is intended to work) must be adapted to the timing of the song. The chorus can be used for humorous redundancies, while the stanzaic part either counteracts it or triggers it in the first place. In short: In music, gags have to be delivered precisely, otherwise they cannot unfold their effect.

As a rule, humorous songs tell stories. The narration of the story must therefore, in order to function in the music, be abstracted to the rhythm of the song and adapt to it.

So far, so good. But what about the broken or served expectations? Actually, this can be explained almost as easily as the dimension of timing. A song usually consists of verses. These verses rhyme at best, so that the pure text of a song has the appearance of a poem. And it is precisely with the topic of "rhymes" that we start with the broken or served expectation.

In the case of the broken expectation, it works like this: A verse builds up a scenario and ends on a word with significance. The following verse tells the scenario onwards and leads to the expected counterpart of the significant word in terms of content. Take the following example: "You can't get the honey." (verse one) "Because you don't have the..." (verse two)

If the word "money" has crossed your mind in the second verse, then you have had exactly the right expectation. In order to use the stylistic device of the breakthrough, you simply use any other word for the three points instead of "money" (preferably without rhyme, maybe "bees") and you will achieve bizarreness or absurdity and thus humour.

On the other hand, the served expectation... What do you say? I do not have to explain them? You can guess? Okay, you are an attentive reader. But let me put it in a nutshell for the not-so-fast ones, too: With the served expectation you simply put "money" for the three points.

There you go. That wasn't so bad, was it? Hey, come back here. The chapter's not over yet. Whatever. I'll just follow you to the next one. I'll see you in a minute.

# Humour in Movies

Got you. Please don't run away from me again. Because now it's about the idiosyncrasies of comic elements in movies. Unlike music, there is another dimension to television: the camera.

Through the camera, the viewer of the funny film is able to perceive things that remain hidden from the protagonists of what they see. For example, we can laugh at people who run to their doom without knowing it. Example: Someone unsuspectingly drives towards the abyss, whistles along the way, is happy, enjoys his life, while we viewers in front of the camera have already been given the image of the abyss and thus have a level of knowledge that eludes the protagonist.

The play with knowledge and ignorance is a humorous element for which I envy the film. Maybe I'll switch and bring the Encyclopædia Comédica to the cinemas as a blockbuster, instead of bringing it to the bookshops as paperback. If you are reading these words right now, instead of watching them magnificently staged on a screen, then unfortunately the financing has not worked out. If you could see me now: I'm clenching my fist in the direction of the producer. This time it's the left, because the right is still affected by the intermezzo with my editor, you remember.

The film has the advantage of being able to make use of almost all the humour elements that exist. He can use memorable jokes, puns, slapstick, frivolities (well, maybe he'd rather not), classic jokes, satire, black humor, etc. All means of comedy are possible for filming.

You know what? I think I have to stop writing about movies, otherwise my displeasure about the failure to finance my blockbuster project will just get worse. Maybe I should save myself into a chapter I feel comfortable with and (I hope) know my way around. Follow me. We are done with movies. Now comes a much better subject.

You do not want to leave yet? You want to know more about humour in films? Oh, just watch all the parts from the Naked Gun on DVD. Think of this as basic study in cinematic humor. A possible postgraduate course would be Mel Brooks. If you are able to understand and analyze High Anxiety and Life Stinks, you can call yourself a Master. And if that's not enough, I recommend the US-American cartoon series Rick & Morty (currently probably the most intelligent and funniest thing there is to "see"). Now let's finally move on to the next chapter. In this one I have home advantage. You'll see.

# Humour in literature

(Satisfied "Ahhh" followed by "Yup, yup, yup, welcome to my second favorite chapter) It's difficult to make the written word so that the reader can laugh heartily about it, believe me. If I have interpreted your behaviour correctly, I have not been able to coax much more from you than grins, smiles and the occasional giggle. What do you say? You laughed? How kind. You didn't have to lie. But thank you.

The challenge of humorous literature is to anticipate the reader's reading speed, intonation and reading interval. Problem: I don't even know you as I write these lines. I don't know whether you need a minute or three for a page. Also, I can't tell if you are actually overemphasizing *italic words* as I do in my head when I write them down. And last but not least, I can't judge whether you read only one page per day or the whole book. As an author, I have to find a way to weigh up the two extremes and find the golden mean, so to speak.

My text must therefore (if it wants to make as many readers laugh as possible) be adjusted to the average. But here we come to the next problem, which I would like to describe with one of my favourite comparisons:

A person whose head is in the oven and whose feet are in the ice has an average temperature of 36.5 degrees Celsius. (Presumably, in your home country, you indicate the temperature in Fahrenheit. In this case, imagine the value 97.7). A healthy value, you might think. However, I would still rate the chances of survival of this person as low. And the same can happen to me with a text. While I try to operate the middle, I sway between one extreme and the other without realizing it.

How can this problem be solved? The answer: Max Mustermann. (This name will not mean much to you. You probably know him more as John Doe) My good Max is 35 years old, has an IQ of 100, goes on vacation twice a year, has 1.4 children and 2.3 cars. He eats three meals a day, goes to the polls every four years and loves watching "M.A.S.H." (Now you got me. This chapter is quite old. Let's just say our Max likes to watch...no idea, what do people watch on TV today? Does that even still exist, or is it just streamed in the meantime? Well, it's not really important for our example, so let's leave this topic )

This Max is an ideal conception, a simplification of reality and thus actually far away from it. And above all (I think I'm starting too many sentences with "and" right now, but never mind.) And above all this Max doesn't correspond to my own character in any way.

I think that we humans are much less empathetic than we think. If we want to hit the tone of a certain person, we usually don't make it, because we are not that person. It is difficult for us to predict what another person wants to read, what he finds funny, what he finds offensive and what he accepts. On the other hand, we often know quite well what we ourselves want to read. And that (my God, again this grotesque "and" at the beginning of the sentence.) And that is my solution to the challenge of comic literature: If you want to write a funny text, write one that you would laugh at yourself. Don't assume what others find funny or interesting. If you think it is funny and worth reading, then maybe others will do the same. Not everyone, but perhaps some people. And these few people (that was now the last sentence with "and" at the beginning, I promise.) And these few people will be grateful to you for choosing authentic words. Because that is what literature is all about. The written word must fit you. It has to be clear that a person has developed the text in his head and not a machine on the drawing board. Because then (wait a minute, these "because"s at the beginning of the sentence are not much better, maybe I'll switch back to the "and" again). And then you create literature that is sincere and that the reader goes along with.

Don't worry about writing badly. In my opinion, nobody can seriously judge what is good writing and what is bad anyway. For example, one person finds The Hitchhiker's Guide to the Galaxy by Douglas Adams hilarious, and another person has absolutely no use for this kind of writing. Some say that Tolstoy's War and Peace is the greatest epic ever written, and some say it's pretentious crap. You will get both positive and negative feedback with everything you write, depending on who you give it to to read. The important thing, in my opinion, is that *you* stand by what you put on paper. If you do that, success will come naturally.

By the way, you can believe one thing. If I had known beforehand how difficult it is to translate a German-language book on comedy into English and to translate it in such a way that it is still (or even at all) funny, I wouldn't have started. But now I've already done more than half of it. At NASA, I think they call this the Point of no Return. That's why I immediately move on to the next chapter. Follow me.

# Humour in computer and video games

And home field advantage again. Besides my work as a book author, I also write stories for computer and video games, so I can tell you that humour is strongly underrepresented in this medium. Well, actually it is not underrepresented, but mostly simply miserably implemented.

At the same time, the medium of games has many more possibilities and dimensions in the field of comedy than music, film and literature together. After all, a game can unite all these things. A good game has good music, good video sequences and good text. What is added (not only with good games, but also with bad games) is the fact of the possibility of interaction. Because you, the player, literally hold the trigger in your hand, you are the one who makes the decisions, and for whom the story of the game is much more personal than if you simply consumed it uninvolved, like your favorite evening television show (sorry, nobody watches that anymore. Just think if I had written "on Netflix, Hulu, Dinsney+ or Amazon" instead of "on TV")

I would like to explain humor in gaming with a concise example: Let's take the role-playing game No One Lives In Heaven.

In this game you travel to a world in which the characters have been left alone for years and have now developed their own will and consciousness. I don't want to bore you with the details, but in one of the quests (missions) you are allowed to write theatre plays. The funny element: You write them and your words are also used, but the actor alienates your input, so that completely different contexts than you planned arise. This alienation alone is funny, but because you are involved in the story and have contributed to its progress, your emotional connection to the story is much stronger than if you had seen the plays in a real theatre, as a mere spectator. Also, depending on how creative you are as a player, the quest is always different, and no two games are the same.

In another quest in No one lives in heaven, you can help a young man win the woman of his dreams. You can either get him a cute pet, which he can then give as a present, or you can pick flowers, which he can bring to his beloved. And here's the funny thing: Instead of handing over the flowers fresh and fragrant, you have the option of doing your bidding on them first. The result: The beloved one thinks both you and the man are idiots and the quest has failed. It was fun anyway, maybe much more so than if you had done it with the pet and the man was now in steady hands.

For a change I would like to give you an example, which is not from No One Lives in Heaven, but from the action shooter RPG "The Outer Worlds". At the beginning you will be given the task of landing on a planet with a space capsule and meeting a contact person so that he can explain everything important to you on the ground. You give this contact the coordinates of your landing point so that he knows where to meet you. Now for the funny part: The contact takes the coordinates *so precisely* that you land not only at him, but *on top* of him. The result: He is dead and your expectation to get everything explained so you can play relaxed is gone. You must discover the peculiarities of the world for yourself. So the humorous element is again linked to your playful interactivity, so that a maximum of immersion is achieved. A film, a book or a song can't achieve such a thing. Only computer games such as The Outer Worlds or No One Lives in Heaven can do this, as they are able to use several media transfer paths and also involve the player in their own narration.

# Humour in other cultures, that's what the world laughs about

This book will be published mainly in German. This is not possible any other way, because most of my shenanigans and low puns cannot be translated and most of the allusions would hardly be understood by non-Germans. I can therefore assume that you either had German as a foreign language at school or as your mother tongue in your life. Your sense of humour is therefore likely to have been influenced by Central Europe. This enables me to talk to you about comedy in other cultures. (I'm sorry, dear English native speaker, but you'll have to get through this now. This chapter was written when I had no intention of translating this book. Let's see if maybe even in this chapter we fail at the project).

Everybody knows the ethnic differentiations like "British humour" (you know it), "Rhenish cheerfulness" (you don't know it), "Viennese taunt" (you don't know it either) or "American comedy" (you know it, in turn). Maybe you have heard sentences like "That's typically British" or "Only Americans can laugh about that."

But is that really the case? British humour is often accused of being dry and riddled with slapstick. Well, *I* can laugh at that too. Rhenish cheerfulness is often very direct and hard, Viennese jokes are often ironic or cynical and American comedy likes puns and situation comedy.

(Don't you? You probably know that much better than I do.)

As you can see, these cultures make use of the same elements of humour that you have already got to know in this book. The only difference lies in their connotation and reference. This, by the way, is the most important insight you can draw from this book. If there is one thing you want to take away from the Encyclopædia Comédica, it is this: The smallest components of a comic entity are universal humour elements. This sounds a bit technical at first, so let me explain it a bit more (At this point, a pun would have come up that is based on the fact that my surname sounds similar to the German word for "explaining". That would have almost been the moment to dismiss the project as a failure, but I will continue. Just imagine if you were German for a moment and could laugh about this bad pun.)

No matter what culture you look into, the structures according to which jokes, sketches, funny situations etc. are built up are always the same. Just as we Germans (or you Americans, English, Australians, etc.) swap syllables to generate word games, so do the French, Russians, Chinese and all those who communicate using language. Asian irony grows out of absurdity just as much as African or European irony, and many a classic joke can be found (in slightly differentiated forms) all over the world.

Of course, only a German can laugh about the delay of the Deutsche Bahn (or as an American about Amtrak's) or the construction time of the BER (you remember, that's the German capital's airport that will never be finished) and only a native speaker can find "Why is six scared of seven? Because seven ate nine" is funny. But me as a non-native speaker and someone who had English in school finds the joke funny, just like an American can find train jokes funny when he visited Germany and "was allowed" to use them. The subjects of the comedy may vary from culture to culture and surely there are also small differences, for example in timing (southern Europeans, for example, like to ignite punch lines earlier, while in the north they spend more time on exposition) and at first glance "foreign humor" may seem completely different from what we know from our home country. But if we look at the basic structures and break them down into their humour elements, we notice that they are the same everywhere.

It seems that humour is not a pure humanistic science, but rather a natural science that can be analysed, understood and applied.

If it wasn't, you probably wouldn't have bought this book either. What other reason would you have had if you hadn't believed that with the right theory, humour can be put into practice and greatly increase the frequency of the laughs you receive? If you apply the principles of this book, you can use them in any country with every stroke of humanity. The only thing you need to consider is the cultural transfer you need to make to abstract the elements to your environment. Once you have done this, you can in principle make the whole world laugh.

# Humour of the future, we will laugh about it the day after

In the course of human history, the basic humour elements have always remained the same. Despite this, we laugh about different things today than people did 100 or even 1,000 years ago. Why is this so? What is the difference between modern and medieval, between contemporary and ancient humour?

I don't want to use this chapter to provide a historical outline of humour through the ages. Probably you can read this topic much better prepared on Wikipedia or other internet sites. You do not need this book for that. Rather, I would like to explain one of my theories to you. I do not claim to be correct, it is rather a disputable assumption. But let me formulate it and then you and I can discuss it.

Hypothesis: We humans have a collective subconscious through which we are all connected to each other. This subconscious stores information from the last millennia and serves today's people as a basis for emotions, decision-making and motivation. Just as this collective subconscious develops further and is subject to a constant gain of knowledge, our humour is also nuanced. The setting and content of humour is still formed by its circumstances and the world and the peculiarities of the time in which it is used.

If you analyse the humour of a certain epoch, it is a condensation of the social, political, economic and cultural conditions (setting and content), consisting of the humour elements you already know and correlating with the state of the collective subconscious.

Let's take, for example, the oldest joke that we humans know. It is about 4,000 years old, comes from ancient Babylon and was found on stone tablets with the following wording: "What has not happened since unimaginable times: A young woman who does not fart on her husband's lap."

Setting and content are due to the time and relatively easy to classify. We can also determine the humor elements used: A mixture of observation, absurdity and broken expectations. Quasi the same ones we already know. Nevertheless, we find it difficult to laugh about the joke, because it obviously (even if we didn't know it before) comes from another (not our own) time.

The joke seems bland, hackneyed and has too few corners to think about. It almost seems as if it was created when we humans did not yet have such a strong (collective-unconscious) sense of humour and could still (like children) be made to laugh with little subtle means.

Let's take a joke for a direct comparison, which will no longer be current when this book is published, but which is all the more relevant now at the moment of writing and can therefore easily keep up with the Babylonians as a testimony of the times.

The US talk show host Conan O'Brien has made the following statement in the course of the separation of England from the EU: "Brexit will make prices go up in Britain, so it will cost them twice as much to not go to the dentist."

Once again, setting and content are clearly defined by the time frame. Everyone knows without research: This is roughly from 2019, and we can find out the humorous elements: A mixture of observation, absurdity and broken expectations. Quasi the same elements as in the joke above. Nevertheless, both seem different (which is not only because the older one is also the more frivolous). In my opinion, we have to make one more abstraction in the Brexit joke than in the young woman on the lap gag. We have to achieve a cognitively higher performance, because the joke has to satisfy our collective unconscious (high) demands.

# Memes, the humour of the Internet, or the new form of allusion

Since the noughties at the latest, memes have become an integral part of youth subculture. Yet they are nothing more than the Internet version of the classic allusion (which in favour of memes did not get its own chapter in this book, what a pity).

With memes and allusions it is similar to humour in other cultures. Basically, they work on the same principles as most jokes and silly things: By comparing, exaggerating, playing with words, observing, etc. However, both presuppose a very specific heuristic in the receiver.

But let's first clarify what a meme actually is. The term was first coined in 1976, when Richard Dawkins in his book "The Selfish Gene" noted that cultural information is disseminated by means of the stylistic device of allusion. In concrete terms, this means that socio-cultural units of consciousness (mems) are humorously prepared and thus become memes. Through the medium of the Internet this is of course possible to a much more intensive and pronounced extent than in the 70s or 80s. Today's memes are usually a picture or video montage in which a largely universally known content is combined with a critical and/or humorous element, thereby creating a meta-level that is only accessible to someone involved in the mentioned cultural phenomenon. However, if either the basis or the abstraction is not present in the heuristic of the recipient, the meme will not work. Thus, the allusion not only fulfils the facts of the silliness, but also serves as a criterion of exclusion for people who do not live in their own filter bubble. The phrase "Get out of my tree house" is thus practically applied. For example, a gamer can test his counterpart for social compatibility with a gaming meme, while railwaymen can achieve this with railway memes and car lovers with PS-strong memes. Each subculture now has its own meme culture, which is often only accessible to like-minded people and thus organically excludes those with different interests.

Surely you know this from your own bubble. Whenever the following sentence comes to your mind while looking at a humorous entity on the Internet, it's a meme shaped by your personal subculture: "Only a real XY can understand that." In this case, the letters XY stand for your personal bubble. Memes do not - as one might think - primarily serve to exclude the undesirable, but rather to identify and confirm the identity of wanted and liked people. After all, our species is a herd and social animal. We do not want to be alone, to share our interests with other parts and to participate in the interaction with other humans. With both of us, you my faithful reader and me, it is the same: We both want to make the world and ourselves a little more fun. Laughter is our bubble and humour our distinguishing feature.

# The humour of humourlessness

They say we Germans are the most humorless people in the world. And you will probably agree with this thesis when you finish this book. But did you ever think that the rest of the world just doesn't understand "our" humor?

Maybe we Germans are funny in a way that is interpreted by other nationalities as humourless. We are regarded as stuffy, serious and dogged. But in our seriousness and stoicism there is nothing but pure absurdity. In this chapter I will introduce you to the supreme discipline of German humour: The humor of humorlessness.

I don't suppose you're familiar with these comedians. I recommend that you enter their names on Youtube and skip in on each one for about a minute. This will give you a good feeling for how their humour works without you having to know the language.

If this is too tiring for you, skip this chapter and watch the South Park episode "Fun bot" instead. It doesn't really do justice to our topic, but it also has something to do with the Germans' lack of humor. Apart from that it's just a good episode.

But enough of beating about the bush. If you're still here, dear reader, we'll start with the actual chapter.

Do you know the DIE PARTEI politician Nico Semsrott? No? Then please Google him, I'll wait here. ...(wait...wait...wait...)

There you are again. And? Have you noticed anything? Exactly! This guy looks like he's depressed and it's funny. But why?

We could (the emphasis is on "could", even if it wasn't written in italics) end this chapter rather quickly by stating that the humour of humourlessness arises from the element of absurdity. After all, we expect a comedian to be funny and accordingly always cheerful and good-humored. Take Otto (a good comparison with an American comedian would be Jim Carrey here), for example, the non-Frisian. His gurgle, which cannot be imitated and is difficult to grasp in letters, is in a way his trademark. We can't imagine Otto being depressed. (Or can you do that with Jim Carrey?) With Nico Semsrott and other depression comedians such as the youtuber Sascha Hellinger this is not the case. They break through our expectations and thus create the comic element.

Otto Julius Bierbaum (also known under the pseudonyms Simplicissimus and Martin Möbius), who died as early as 1910, already recognized in the last century: "Humor is when you laugh anyway." The condensation and reflection of actually depressing and devastating statements, in connection with minimalistic facial expressions and phonetics, causes bizarreness and laughter about the turmoil of the world. Everybody knows situations in which everything simply goes wrong, nothing wants to succeed and it seems as if the universe has conspired against you. Exactly in such moments we don't know whether we should cry or laugh. As I said: humour is when you laugh anyway, even if we actually don't feel like laughing due to the circumstance. Those are exactly those laughs, which are followed by sentences like "Well, actually it's not funny" or "Ui, that one was bad" and which we like to sort into the category gallows humor.

Let's take another concise example for the supposed conclusion of this humorless chapter. Best of all, one by the aforementioned Nico Semsrott: If you have followed the European elections of 2019, you may have noticed the advertising clip of the party DIE PARTEI. In this clip, the depressed Nico is standing in a hospital, his dark hood pulled over his head, his hands pressed against his body. In the background you can see old people, whose further life expectancy is presumably to be indicated in days instead of years. Nico Semsrott says in mono tone: (Disclaimer: my own choice of words follows, after all I don't want to take ideas out of the mouth of good Nico). "Here you can see a so-called last voter. He is allowed to decide about a future he will not experience himself. Unfair! The solution: If you can't vote in the first 18 years of your life, you shouldn't be allowed to vote in the last 18 years either."

(Actually I could have left out the quotation marks. They were my own words anyway. Too bad I don't have a tipper ex.) You can see that Nico Semsrott likes it morbid, but in the core he is right. Actually, this should be depressing. Nevertheless most of the audience laughed and the clip went viral. It's the gallows humor, the humor of humorlessness, that forms the comedy in this case.

By the way, this kind of humor also works when the reference to reality is more difficult to comprehend or even gets completely out of place. Comedian Markus Maria Profitlich once scored with the sentence: "My parents were so poor. The only cake I got was the placenta." Sorry, I should have left that joke out. In German, the word placenta is made up of the words mother and cake. But I see that despite my explanation, you're not laughing. It's probably not your humor. But believe me, when he threw that sentence on his show Mensch Markus, the audience roared. We know that the mini-anecdote is not true, nevertheless it works (in German).

# Humor from the other star, aliens laugh about it

Now he's gone completely mad, you'll think. You already knew at the preface that this Leuteritz has lost his marbles. And if he still has them all, then at least not in the right order or color. Either way, you will have thought about me latently while reading. Now you have certainty: Leuteritz is writing a chapter about aliens. If you want, you can go to the bookstore with your book and your sales receipt, refer to the title of this chapter and ask for your money back. It will probably work...

Please don't do this. I really just want to start a thought experiment with you. Let's not talk about real aliens, let's talk about things that transcend us humans. Allow me to ask a few questions, just think in the bag, as they say, let's see where they lead:

How does humor work in the fourth dimension? What would a quantum computer laugh at if it had consciousness? Do smartphones make fun of us behind our backs because we think we are using them as tools, but in reality it's the other way around? How would humour work if effect and cause were reversed (first the punch line, then the derivation)? What would we find funny if time was running backwards instead of forwards? Are there species where laughter is bad and grief is good? Can bacteria and viruses feel joy? Would an alien interpret human laughter as a bizarre malfunction? Can lack of humor be treated medically? Is this even a recognized disease or even disability? By how many years less does a person who never has fun live compared to one who is constantly enjoying himself? Are we humans just extras of a divine comedy? What does God laugh at? Does he laugh at all? Is there a parallel universe where laughter was never invented? Would we humans still be funny even if we lacked the physical ability to laugh, that is, if humor could only be expressed in our heads? Is it possible to laugh so much that humor is lost forever? Is the Earth the only planet where laughter exists, or is it perhaps the most humourless of the animated universe? Is Pennywise also a funny clown or can he only be evil? What did cavemen find funny? And last but not least, probably the most hackneyed classic of all humorous questions: Do you die if you laugh half to death twice?

One could certainly write several dozen books about all these questions (except maybe the last one) without getting even an inch closer to the truth. Nevertheless, I find each one exciting. Okay, this chapter may have less to do with aliens than the title suggests. But the alternative title "May I ask you a question?" unfortunately didn't appeal to me that much. I wanted it more lurid. After all, you're supposed to read the chapter.

If you have paused to think about any of the above questions for even a moment, then you and I are of the same mind. We want accurate answers to vague questions. We're dreamers, visionaries, aesthetes...

Okay, okay, all right. I know I'm exaggerating. We're not *that* kind of dreamers. But sometimes I like to let my thoughts flow and see where they lead. Maybe nowhere, maybe somewhere. And if you flow too far, I'm happy to have a reader like you to wake me up and bring me back to reality. Thank you for that. Without you, I would have gotten lost in this chapter, maybe even in the whole book.

# A few words about the English edition

I must admit that the translation was fun. Therefore I would like to give you - dear English-speaking reader - this exclusive chapter as a gift, which was withheld from the Germans.

By the way, I can easily afford this chapter, because your language is in comparison to mine about 10% shorter, respectively more compact. Most German words are very long and bulky, while in English you use rather short, concise (and also cool) words.

So it is possible for me to add many additional ideas as well as to write a complete additional chapter, and still get the same page number as in the German version.

While we are on the differences between our two languages. Did you know that there are many German words for which there is no equivalent in English and vice versa? For example, we have a word for when you can't get a song out of your head. We call it earworm (literally translated). In addition, children are sometimes colloquially called "three cheeses up" and if someone is forced to do something, he or she is under "Zugzwang" (there is not even a literal translation for this word. It is unfortunately much too different from the English language in terms of its structure). The same is the case with our word "Weltschmerz". The literal translation of world pain does not quite do justice to the meaning that someone feels all the injustice in the world in a depressive state.

In contrast, we Germans are not able to translate narrow terms like low-brainer, underbelly or doggy bag. In our language there is simply no equivalent.

I hope that you enjoyed the English version of this book and that my knowledge of your mother tongue did not disturb you too much, so that you could enjoy reading it.

The following chapter (although the term chapter may not be appropriate for an afterword) is again written for all language families.

# Afterword humour / Epilogue comedy / Closing gag

Dear reader, I must ask you a very important question and I want you to answer it honestly. Believe me, I would know if you were lying. Have you really read the book up to this point and not already turned to the bookstore for the final word to see how it ends? Okay, fine, I believe you. Then it's time for me to make a confession: I wrote that book for the money. Actually, I don't care if you enjoyed it, if it got you anything, or if it lived up to your expectations. The only thing that really matters is that you (or the person who gave it to you) spent money on it.

Sure, I know what you're going to say: "Bookwriting doesn't make any money these days." Let me tell you the following: 1. I would type book writing as two words and 2. there are two branches of literature that are still commercially successful: guidebooks and humorous books. It's true that bad advice is often expensive (I've already spent over 30€ for such a "get your life together" book) and funny stuff is sometimes just embarrassing (for example when 80-year-old authors think they know how to use youthful colloquial language).

But I've heard that with a guidebook you can easily sell a few thousand copies. But that's not enough for me. With funny books, you can easily scratch 10,000 copies. My quintessence: You are now reading a funny guidebook. That easily brings me to ten and a few thousand books sold. Thanks to you, for example! Thanks to what? My book didn't give you any useful advice? Anyway, that still leaves the 10,000. What's that? It's not funny either? Now, look... I thought we'd become friends over the last 40,000 words. Or were you faking it? If you did, you were damn good at it. Because I hadn't noticed. But you know what? I don't really care if you found my book funny or educational, you paid for it anyway. Didn't you? What are you talking about? You lied? You're actually standing in the bookstore right now, just flipping to the end? I don't believe this. Now you've applied the principle of subtextual wit. If you want to know what that is, I guess you'll have to start at the beginning after all. Ha, ha. Ha-ha-ha. I beg your pardon? You skim to that chapter in a hurry and skim? Well, that's a bit much. You know something? I'll have the chapter titles removed by the publisher before the book goes to press. You'll look stupid. What? It's already in print? And the chapter titles are there too? If you'll excuse me, I have to go talk to my publisher...

# After the afterword

Actually, the first epilogue should already be serious. With all those platitudes like "I'm glad you had time to read my book", "I hope you enjoyed it", "Maybe we'll meet again in the next book" and all that Poppycock. But somehow I can't seem to stay serious. I think I've gotten to grips with humour so intensively now that I can't stop. That's why I'm going to pull myself together, straighten up, as the saying goes, and say to you from the bottom of my heart: I'm glad you had the time to read my book. I hope you enjoyed it. Maybe we'll meet again in the next book."

What do you mean, you can't take these sentences seriously? Poppycock?! Did I really write this? All right, I did, but I didn't mean it. Let's not part on bad terms. I had a great time with you. To be honest, you were the best reader I ever had. (By the way, I heard you just whisper "and the only one" But I don't blame you. You just learned a lot from my book and now you're a funny and witty person)

If you apply, practice and perfect everything you just read in your everyday life, I promise you that the people around you will laugh (positively) at you from now on. Used correctly, you will succeed in calming screaming babies, taking the wind out of the sails of screaming colleagues or detoxifying the screaming bureaucracy of narrow-minded clerks. I remember when I founded my company SuR ENTERTAINMENT. My business partner and I went to the trade office in Leipzig, took a number, were called up instantaneously (another waste of uprooted trees) and sat opposite a sternly looking clerk who greeted us politely as follows: "What do you want?" and looked at us (okay, I admit it, I wore sweatpants and didn't necessarily look like a professional company founder) critically from top to bottom. It was clear to me: If I don't make a joke immediately, the concentrated power of German bureaucracy will strike us, including Asterix and Obelix's A38 permit. I looked around frantically and my gaze remained glued to the calendar. Perfect, I thought, and said: "Today is a recognized lucky day after all. That's why we want to start a happy company. The woman first frowned, then also looked at the calendar and then (relievingly) started to laugh. My business partner and I joined in. The conversation then became very pleasant and the editor gave us many useful tips, which I know are only given to selected (because friendly) people. Even our company name became better than we had originally intended thanks to my joke, because the editor thought along with us and had the better ideas thanks to her greater experience. To be honest, I believe that we were the first company founders to which this woman showed so much interest and help. Humorous people just get ahead and are appreciated everywhere. Those who make people laugh earn their sympathy. By the way, the date on which we founded the company was a 13th. Now you know that joke wasn't even good. It still worked. How much will your jokes work then, which, with the knowledge of this book, will have the ability to make diaphragms burst? Rhetorical question. They will work so well that you won't even blame me for promoting my computer games company in the closing words of this book. Reminder: SuR ENTERTAINMENT. You just finished reading a book. This is a perfect time to google this funny SuR, don't you think?

# This is (not) an acknowledgment

Did you know I hate thank-you notes? I mean, let's be honest. The only people who read such things are the people named in them as well as the author himself and maybe his editor. With great authors, at best, the publishing house management takes another look at it. All others skip the "chapter", which doesn't really deserve the name and finish the book at the latest after the epilogue or epilogue. Acknowledgements offer no added value.

Maybe my aversion to printed expressions of gratitude is also due to the fact that I myself have never been mentioned in one. Whenever I *actually* read through a thank-you note, I felt like an uninvolved voyeur watching the great writer pat the back of people I've never heard of and (if I avoid future thank-you chapters) I'll never hear of again.

Call it envy, but I don't like acknowledgments. This is information about me which I hope you will not even notice, since you have already read through your Encyclopædia Comédica and put it aside with a pleasant feeling. The only people who get to read my last words (funny expression, I should change it) are probably the very ones who are frowning, because their name is not mentioned as expected. All I can say is: Take that, you agents, editors, wives and husbands, children, parents, hamsters and guinea pigs, or whoever (actually) deserves to be named here. This is what it feels like when you read acknowledgements in which you are not mentioned. I bet you feel bad now.

And now that I've scared away the only people who are listening to me now (although this word seems out of place in a book), I should close my soliloquy. But before I do this (a word my German teacher hated, because in our language this auxiliary verb is only used when you can't think of the more appropriate main verb; so I guess I have scared him away now, too), I would like to take the opportunity to express my sincere thanks to everyone who meets the world with laughter instead of malice, with fun instead of anger, and with humor instead of seriousness.

*By the same author:*

"Die Hütte - Chronik eines Mörders" published by Books on Demand (9,99€ as paperback and 5,99€ as eBook)

Where is the border between imagination and reality? What if you can no longer distinguish between the two? What if reality and imagination suddenly change places and a roller coaster ride into the abyss of your own psyche begins for you, at the end of which there is no way back? Maik Beyer suffers from schizophrenia after a traumatic experience in his past. Again and again, backflashes haunt him, to the point where the past completely consumes him and in the present he forces the woman of his dreams to love him. In an abandoned cabin she languishes her agonizing martyrdom. Who can stop Maik's bloody path? To conquer the beautiful Jennifer, he has to eliminate all enemies one by one...

*By the same author:*

"No one lives in heaven"
Video game by SuR ENTERTAINMENT

What happens to the characters in a game world after you have "played through" it? Let's take any role-playing game. Usually the game world is threatened by an evil power and a hero (almost always the player) has to save it by solving main and side quests. If he has made it to the end credits, there is usually an uninstall or a start over (with the same evil power and the same human-written quests). No one lives in heaven is also such a game. At least it used to be, many years ago. Players have travelled the 5 continents of the game world, defeated bosses and solved puzzles. Today you are the first person to experience No One Lives in Heaven in the year 2020 and step into a world where NPCs have been left alone. Equipped with free will and creative subroutines, they began to question their existence. They fathomed their meaning and realized that they were nothing more than digital game pieces without physical existence. You are now the one who decides their future.

This is the end of the book.

You can stop reading now.